Tim Murphy

MOUTH OF SHADOWS

SurVision Books

First published in 2022 by
SurVision Books
Dublin, Ireland
Reggio di Calabria, Italy
www.survisionmagazine.com

ISBN: 978-1-912963-29-4

For Gerard Staunton

Acknowledgements

Grateful acknowledgement is made to the editors of the following, in which some of these poems, or versions of them, originally appeared:

Beir Bua Journal: "Perpignan," "Figment of Silence," and "Psilocybin"
Eratio: "In Dreamsight" and "Cairo Calling"
Gegner: "In a Recurring Dream"
Maintenant: "Mouth of Shadows"
Otata: "Backing Vocal"
The Other Bunny: "Mulberry Man"
Otoliths: "The Cacti Do Not Move" and "Every Sunrise"
Sulfur: "Hidden Bow", "Injured Beach Star," "The Great Ships," and "Apple Graves"
SurVision: "Collage Scent," "Mosaic," "Chiang Mai," "The Water Fire," and "The Red Poppies Run to Us"

Thanks to Gerard Staunton and Charlie Baylis for invaluable advice on manuscript drafts; and for other encouragement and support during the writing of this book, thanks to Adrian Hunt, Ana Isabel Lozano, Anne MacFarlane, Damian Reardon, Jeffrey Parkey, Joseph Barrett, José Luis de Prado Higueras, Kristin Ketelslegers, Mary Doherty, Michael Staunton, Migle Laukyte, Patrick Hannon, Sergio Peraire Tena, Vincent O'Connell, and Virginia San Felipe Rodríguez.

CONTENTS

I. Between the Eyelids

II. Spring Body Freefall Dance

III. Kaleidoscope Whisper

IV. Easy to Find

I.

Between the Eyelids

Instrumental

Sunday again.
A sombre sculpture moves
through a highway underpass.
An empty studio is fractured
by a pious sunbeam.
A transit landscape shifts itself
to reveal a new absence,
a new marginalization.
The city prints
another symbolic engine.
Sunday again!

Collage Scent

Who is hiding the past well
and who is not?
A woman is ranking her children;
she does not answer.
A hint? An epilogue?
Has a taste been overheard?

Objects roll through
the half-light.
Is this the undertow
or is it the vernal equinox?
The breach is empty
and someone says,
"This is what the past
will look like."

There is talk
of identity dramas
and recognition plots
but no one looks
in the mirror.

When everything is found,
what can be concealed?
The smart money?
A family fracture?

Burning Luggage

Summer flicks her hair
like a switch on the back
of an evil flower.
The carousel speaks in a language
of basslines and falling rocks.
An onscreen car crash collides
with real roadkill.
Divine shadows assemble,
flapping like shredded leather.
Lifeblood seeps through
the burning luggage.
Forecourt taxis blossom
into a swarm of locusts.
Summer hides in the long grass,
dead on her feet.

The Cacti Do Not Move

A blue sepia shone somewhere in the monochrome of the apartment building, while mystic words about spiral life cycles seemed oblivious to the fact of our anaesthetic love heading for the rocks. I remember one of the green birds in your dream spoke of breaking the dawn and opening wide the gates of day, while my dream was of sacraments passing through trees and willow shavings hanging on wands as first snow offerings. It seems a spell was cast dialectically by the two dreams, at least that's the most plausible explanation for what happened in subsequent days and weeks. It was most likely this dialectic, for example, that prompted us to become our own winter secret. The dialectic theory would also explain the background cello sounds veering constantly into a ghost of a chance that either dream would recur. Ultimately, the whole situation, not least our spiralling arrangements in that apartment, took on a shade of tragedy blue. In fact, that was the blue sepia effect in the monochrome of the building. As regards the dissociated mantras, they have never been explained fully; perhaps a sacrament somehow passed through a day gate, or perhaps a life cycle melted into snow. What else is there to say? The death of our love, by convention I suppose, to nature belongs—but let's not forget, as a kind of addendum to that, that in our dream dialectic the dancers let go and then, suddenly, the cacti do not move, nor do we.

Autumn

At the night gate the sense
of contrasting patterns.

The moment when I decide to stay
eludes me.

The heart is an answer,
like a dead flower
tilting toward the edge of something spare,
something not urban or even complex.

I tell you again I love you—
you reply
with an argument
from tradition.

The patterns merge
without synthesizing,
marking a point in space
that hums before disappearing.

Urbanization

The shapes moving in the morning mist
are festivities without root or error,
their ebbing pageantry fades all crests,
pebbles all outbursts. Light stretches
along the top of the underworld,
forming an indelible question mark.
Many days cry out for recognition
but they cannot be heard.
Each glorious ruin abides alone
and each pawnshop stands its ground.
Cobbled squares open wide their veins,
invoking dahlia, daffodil, dandelion.

Eating with Regret

Night begins, night ends.

Several ideas later, there is movement.
It feels like eating with regret.
Which images appear?
The blindfolded woman's balancing act?
The flickering loneliness machines?
Cargo honey lining the sunset trail?
No! Nothing like that.

Only a mounted canvas,
completely blackened,
seething with the suggestion
of being knifed—

and you, standing there,
for years and years,
blade in hand
until the cut—

only this image brings repose.

You have blunted all the swords,
you have abandoned all the myths.
There's no heyday,
no place to snap out of.

Fear of Memory

Fear of memory violence, memory of
violent fear. Wounded rocks fall
from jagged cliffs. In the distance
I notice you, call to you. The waves
are too loud until, when I call you again,
you hear me. Together, we lift
the ocean's skin, with memory,
with fear. The violence is close at hand.
In the space between you and me
time is collapsed, eclipsed.
I was there, too, with you.
Now it is time for us both
to close the ocean, to go home,
to live.

Hidden Bow

While I rise from the chest of certainty
that teases my eyes,
I am as quiet as a naked arm.
The bright light
flashing between my teeth
troubles me more severely
than your knocked-down story.
I kiss you
between the eyelids,
you, the most beautiful of all.
Overhead,
a piano drowns
and you kiss my music.
Your lips keep my balance
against the dawn.
Ignore the dead water,
forget your sinking harp.
This squared-off paleness
is the shape of two skins.
I do not know
if the sky's hidden bow
sees what strength
it takes for me
to say a few bright words
to the shining dawn.
Why do you keep insisting
when you know I can't respond?
I deny everything.

Backing Vocal

He was your common or garden convent wizard,
always in a patchouli-coloured dance coat.
Northern scenes played out
as he whispered time's tune
in the ears of the future,
and the old song,
all day his shadow would sing it—
Trailer for sale or rent,
Rooms to let, fifty cents—
because of the poverty
and because of the cigarettes.

The jaguar gods watched
as folded grief flags flew freely
in that convent,
and the old song,
the wizard's shadow would really get into it—
No phone, no pool, no pets,
I ain't got no cigarettes . . .

Now, at the junction of it all,
I hear the battle horns
sounding and circling,
I hear the drumbeats
from the floating city,
and the old song,

I can still hear the shadow singing it—
I'm a man of means by no means,
King of the road . . .
Why didn't I throw my dark suit
under a train?

Injured Beach Star

The sand says to the cork float,
"I am where the retreating sea
stores up fossils
in a pink vapour.
When you were a child
I crafted standing stones
that flashed out
in all directions.
In the glancing light,
along the dynamited mountain,
every dazzling thing
is reputed to have dried
into the ether."

And the cork float says to the sand,
"Shapes, with eyes half shut,
stretch out to dismember
the padlocked caves.
Tempest eggs stream out
as if by enchantment.
To rediscover
the immemorial deity's
castoff limbs
or its spine
of incandescent thorns,
it is necessary
to caress
the cliff's edge."

But the shepherd says,
"Memories of childhood,
polished by kelp,
may cajole like a cat within.
The silver bullet,
with its myriad
of closed minds,
rebounds
with a dizzying thrill.
Injured beach star!
Upraise yourself
like an effigy
with an electric smile
and cry out obsessively
towards the trees lit from within!"

The Tipping Point

Take the days of supertramping in the lagered rain,
of weighing each other's gold in blood, or take
the oak tree we understood, the hallucination
we made it become. Remember the portable
passages of time, the prairie peninsulas
and the pagan ports, or when Hilma af Klint
came to us in dreams, as the fruit of a long experience,
allowing us circles from the future . . .
        We are indeed all godlike,
but mythology can become a satellite of betrayal,
and even if the treasure is always closer than we think,
and always waiting to be found, inhabited spirits
cannot know this. Only the tipping point is known:
hangmen rarely lie, and they do not avoid symmetry.

II.

Spring Body Freefall Dance

The Great Ships

One summer night,
under a radiant transit,
my voice was born.
It was born like an enraged wind
made of flesh.
This sobbing head, this tender stone—
an open lobe that dawns
like a dolphin.

Your name was a shadow
between two medallions,
your cry of love
was the same as mine.
Now I'm all alone,
talking with your smile.
In front of me, arriving,
the usual certainty.
A hope is going to shove the moon
out to sea.

The great ships are without limits,
like hollow skin and trampled air.
Waves that mean nothing
roll around in the light.
The shoreline is a caress,
suffering without trying.
Happiness,
restrain your sullied foot.

Minotaur in Green

*"Offre ta gorge à la nuit
Obsédante Afrique..."*

*["Offer your throat to the night
Obsessive Africa..."]*

—Joyce Mansour, "Pandémonium"

offer your blade to the day
sententious Ireland
excrete your dirt your life
your blindness
in the exotic bowl
of the town

the bull's cluster
cuts its shame
with fragile desire
from the black fire extracts a judgement
a cross to bear
a new thrill like the dying days
of a plea
the rain the rain with a cow's heart
hungry projections

the land's erotic veil
claims the field
demands the deed
of your big man act
look no further than the excited bullock's
fluid bewitching
be stubborn like the sun
but cold like a diamond

the suffering
the sorrow pilled up with joy
the tumescent life
love's account book
laughs as rich as gravy
proxies and unsaid words
the smiling cheeks of flushes never felt

exiled families
preachy Ireland
murdered brothers
low hill mist
like a selective story
all pray while dreaming
under the fuchsia shoulder
under ox aggression
all-persistent
oily
quick to surrender

take pins and needles
sear them anew on an open-toothed grave
the minotaur's brain swells
becomes a vehicle
packed and poignant
the weather whips your torture chambers
vicious Ireland
your withered liberty
your bit part in Europe's decay

alive yet
the body abused like a bus seat
tears in spiral staircases
it was yesterday
play interrupted
the silence
unseen
no telescope would query it
the long face
the plaintive scream
the sad alcoholic excuse
dusk's scent of woodsmoke

tomorrow and tomorrow
sanctimonious Ireland
death
between mud and the rising roar
the vagina and the wildflower
the failing light vomiting in the street

intimate possession
intimate control
the lost humility
the cold empathy
dancing in the bullring
dry sand sly sand
unresolved

my life remembers an old hope
a slaughtered story
in the dark of a departure lounge
all I expect is what I can carry
just an image of something sweet
that teases and turns
like a fog image in a mist
all I hear is the music
the rising tide of notes
heavenly life

worse to close the door
the door that is not a door
worse to live dead
than to possess nothing
cry fuckers
you chose not to listen
is this a dagger
that waits?

The Aurochs

for Tinna Ingvarsdóttir

Every week at a certain hour
On a certain day
I float in a sea of floating women.

The sea is clear—
In the shallow parts
You can see
Right through the water—
And every week at the same hour
On the same day,
As I float in this clear sea,
I paint universal circles,
Universal doorways:
I paint mandalas.

All the women are painting, too,
Painting as they float in the clear sea,
Painting maps with shorelines,
Territories with vegetation,
Tigers, angels and graves:
They paint the windows of their pain.

Every week at the same hour
On the same day,
When we float and paint in the clear sea,
These women and I,

We are all copying the pictures
Of the wild cattle on old cave walls;
We are all painting the bison, the wild bulls,
We are all painting the aurochs.

We paint for luck in the hunt,
We paint to cope with our trauma,
We paint our ritual need.

We paint windows of pain and we paint mandalas—
We paint the aurochs.

Speak in Tongue

Burn the hard bones
Extract the charcoal
Tint the cave wall
Shape a free circle

Blow the long horn
Make the wild move
Strike the right note
Play the song smooth

Green the scarred sea
Act the funny part
Dance the new jive
Weave a strong heart

Hammer the hot steel
Strike the halftone
Hum the happy tune
Lay the capstone

Shade the colour in
Bang the big drum
Sculpt the true thing
And speak in tongue

Bound Composition

The soft rock
surprises my throat,
I bruise in blue.

While it kisses your belief,
the rock curves in leather,
a wavering leather.

Blue surprises leather,
the wavering leather,
with clouds of eyes.

The ruined curves
are kissed and soft,
hot like bruised belief.

The soft rock
curves the clouds,
it ruins the blue.

The hot throat
of wavering leather
surprises our eyes.

Reverie for André Breton

My spouses and my lovers were long gone. I had long ago relinquished all my hopes and all my fears. My children had become forest people. The idea of prey was to me anathema; all was shadow, all was spiral surrender. I lived on pathways. I toiled with, and for, love.

But one day, for no apparent reason, I lost my memory. Naturally, and with wine and bread never-ending, I set out to find it. I had an idea of what I was looking for, but no recollection. The idea ate the bread, drank the wine, tried to remember. It was to no avail.

Years later, during a séance of which I had no expectation, my idea's desire to remember revealed itself to be prey disguised as good disposition. Once again, I relinquished everything. This time forever. As an alternative I began juxtaposing coincidences, right here, between these parallels.

Mulberry Man

Lying discarded beneath urban undergrowth, near a mulberry tree, a man is discovered bisecting a dream or an insect— it's not clear which because the man has hijacked his own unconscious mind.

In the dream an insect wakes to reality as a scorpion approaches the dreamer. Outside lies the humidity of a jungle and the sound of crickets. The dreamer is decisive and a death-coloured heel bears down on the scorpion's skull. Danger dies and the dreamer wakes as a discarded man lying near a mulberry tree.

This sense of being discarded haunts the man during his convalescence. How did he come to be beneath the urban undergrowth near the mulberry tree? And why does he still feel as if his mind has been split in two? He writes a poem about an insect— a scorpion— who dreams of a second life.

In Dreamsight

swordfish fight with joy
like windmills crucifying
a dried-out horizon

fallen plum trees
lie like dragons
on bone-dry earth

vast satellites cast
tent awning shadows
over lakes of liquid stone

a dry waterfall
wages war
on a square sand dune

a glazed river
flows through
parched clay

and on a dusty tightrope
an amphibian drowns
in empty space

Spatula in Hand

Spatula in hand I have no fear,
I am astride my vision—
in turpentine mornings
I'd scutter and crawl for it.

I cut into the fusion,
the patterns cut back—
hear the rhymes on canvas,
the half-rhymes on wood.

I step back from the sound,
my heart watches my heart—
shapes arrive out of lines,
colours holler their names.

Oil moves to its own meter,
the sunlight glints with gold—
my vision invites me along,
spatula in hand I have no fear.

Painted Canvases

A hint of ochre, like an infinity symbol,
Like a wide range of options.
Space is an age, time is a vessel.
Too joyful to consider, I have
Painted all the canvases, and yet. A masked
Compass shows the way. I measure
These things, height, depth, weight,
But I don't know where the razor
Is placed. It is the pain of confusion,
The sequence untitled and coming to fruition.
If I do not hesitate, it's so you'll renege.

Birds of Prey

Night's hard shoulder. Dazed, we act out
Into a composition of parody and pain.
Notice what we've compressed.
Anger at the recurrence,
The detour of a concept.

We are in a portrait of the present,
Made warm by humanity
And dispersed like a sieve of light.

Humming along nicely, we each become
A bird of prey, you a black eagle,
I a western osprey.

Withdrawn thus by waking reality
City streets conduct us like copper wire,
Yet we block ourselves at every turn.

A shadow-check in the sun,
A spoken word in the thicket,
A quick end to each new day.

The Moat

Logic's rain falls,
naked to the touch.
The vesper bells incite
while the redbrick moon and hummingbirds
stay silent.

Jupiter and Venus share a joke
by the high-rise vegetation,
something about a double agency bind—
the fairy lights on the bridge
are broken but alive.

Saturn watches the rhythm
of the vaulting night;
he stretches, brushes his teeth.
The next two waves
will make all the difference.

Fleet

a fleet of visions sail
around the rock
of your unconscious mind—
they reverse discarded logic
and confirm that the magic
is indeed in the object
you think it is in—
how many years
in survival mode
has it been?—
have you not grasped
the geography
of the chamber?—
is this the cold calm crisis
that could save you?

Mosaic

Spring body freefall dance, an elevator mosaic
In Naples, somewhere near the train station;
It is August, the day of another circus parade,
No parties, no prayers, only needles in the arm;
No words of love, only boundaries
Bumping into each other, lines of control
Moving around earth's corners, sleeping animals
Looking for any kind of comfort they can find—
The mind moves forward, it builds new mountains,
But like everything under the sun, it is divided;
Let it slip inside shadows, inside renovations,
Take the speedway and press fast-forward:
Search the stone, search the linen canvas,
Find the spring body freefall dance.

III.

Kaleidoscope Whisper

Mouth of Shadows

The body stores
what it cannot forget
in the mouth of shadows.

The psyche builds a maze
with walls of blood.

There are childhood tears in the water,
candy floss clings to each particle of air.
The camera sweeps ahead,
toys are strewn across the lighthouse path,
a lifetime's possessions are piled up in the hall.

Spools of thread gather
like the mystery of sleep,
orgies of self-compassion fight back
tides of imputation.

Inside the hollow-jawed sea,
in every ground swell,
identities are confiscated,
brains are rewired.

In the mouth of shadows
meadow approaches paddock.
Faded grandeur and meretricious love
ambush anything that moves.

Viscosity

The oils await a gilded guideline,
a canvas mark to believe in.
The figure inspires like muslin
primed with chalk—
the petal eyes, the stem neck,
the absence of age.

There's talk along easel ridge,
gossip about the found frame,
but it's merely a dawn defect,
gauze from the other side.
Calm is restored with new poise,
with pinked skin.

It is timely, this ritual air,
this infinite-loop nostalgia.
The brush drags its heel,
it carries an abacus.
The model's gaze carries
all the terrestrial conveys.

Perpignan

Transient ghosts cope with the paradox
of knowing how to handle flaws
by killing off costive thinking
with a merciful sensation streak
and reminding themselves of Perpignan,
its walls and waiting rooms,
its backstreet baptisms,
its slowly exploding border . . .

The fears of things
were still unconscious then,
all of life a bright trance.
But now Perpignan has spoken.
Death is delayed.
The hoofbeats of raw material
issue invitations
like eyes.

Every Sunrise

The sky is a parchment and yearning shuts down the sunset. Soft gusts carry me down rural trails. I call to a woman in a disclosed mansion. She meets me on layers of moving grass and her hands are like bubbles in whitewater rapids. She says, "Clear warning chants ascend the cathedral bell rope yet the misguided flee the forest carriages and the hunted retreat into dry seas."

I meet the woman again while I am walking through a river valley. She appears on the riverbank and this time her hands are aflame. She holds her arms in the air, the flames starting from her wrists, and says, "When you walk in the tracks of the Way, old age leaves the village like a wolf, insects seek rewards in the stillness, and bloodstones release numbers quietly."

The woman and I take to the byways; we get to know the land. At sad moments, we speak thoughts happily. A pattern is soon established: every sunset sadness and happiness converge, and every sunrise we find objects already in our possession.

Apple Graves

There is no cure for craving
the open mouths of dying canyons.
It is useless to look
through the shadowy faucets
of magnifying glasses—
even obscure names frighten
the vigilance of the night.
Landscapes full of graves
yield tiny apples
because of a silence
that has no roots.
The violent moon attacks
the entire arch of the sky.
Facades of smoke
wait in ambush
for a single corpse.
It does not matter
if we must journey
where equilibrium
loses its way.

Barricades of Pain

I wandered into a cannonade of nations.
I saw lamps of democracy and wings of liberty.
I saw a crown, a cross, and a spear.
There was Hellenic delight and anarchist passion.
There were Christs, boy-priests, and soldiers.
The children of kings remained
shamed and dissonant,
like the wildest oranges retreating
before the daring of snow.

God knows how far the spray
of the holy bloody sun
will overhang the flowers of Genoa,
God knows how long each bright bird
will sound a discreet cry of dull woe.
A blossom moon fills inviolate rights
with waves of terror.
Narcissi drown in a bay
of treacherous months.
The curved green weeks cannot save
the bitter sea.

They have slain the soul of my brother,
they have robbed his young brain.
His eyes roar and rage
but the hour of his reign has passed.
What has been written
has burned and died.

Overload

A butterfly flutters through an overcrowded world,
it watches people play strip poker for a dime,
fleeting knots of love deepen,
hope remains a whore of time.

There's torture on the tattoo terrace
and ladyboy love in the lounge,
the madam's embroiled in a commotion,
dissent starts to sound a bit strange.

On the horizon workers gather,
in the alleyway there's a parade,
but the machines are all dialectic
and taboo is way out of range.

Beneath the wheel a voice cries out for help,
trying to get a taste of what's good,
but there's a feel of stonework solitude
about a coffin's cradling wood.

The Here and Now

The mind is a question,
a sense of unknowing.
You showed me yours,
I showed you mine.
We endured that way for years,
choices unmade,
torn away from the light.

I went underground to resist,
sleeping recklessly,
transgressing carefully.
You kicked curiosity
into touch,
calculating a response
and dividing it
by an archway to lesser decisions.

There are no ways back
into the conundrum,
no ways to heed again
the howl of reason's rage,
the clack of bitter love
twisting and turning
in the magma of the night.

The circles are full,
our spells spent.

Change and desire
no longer intersect.
This is the here and now.
Our minds are without defence
against the world.

Projection

I have labyrinth intuition worship,
vital monster regeneration,
action symphony legacies.

You have vinyl destiny planets,
congealed brownstone seas,
original excursus devotion.

We can turn down the music
and cook up a still life
with an octopus and galloping red horses,
we can plan for a citizens' banquet
as part of a formula for spring,
there can be grand glove gestures
and there can be fire falling free.

Frame it as the decay of an elementary dream
or as a quiet watershed,
but killing ghosts are weaving through the dream canals,
microdot marriages are crying out
for some mean time, some screen time,
some me time and some manic-phase time . . .
Oh yes, believe it, the fantasia is real.

Figment of Silence

A biomorphic abstraction frames an application
that keeps repeating itself.
The environment is limited. Dense.
A server programs a closed source.
The presence of gaps in the platform
seems authentic, reassuring.

All at once six sides of mortar
lodge
in the cornerstone's memory,
dowelled mallets
chisel in rotation
around a French drag straightedge,
ashlar trowels
point the way
to the tuck rubble—
it's an obscene carving frenzy,
like a kaleidoscope whisper
among cathedral shadows.

A monitor network scans
a binary icon.
Lakes of data disappear
into a collapsed update.
The platform wobbles,
it reboots a blank page.
A kernel link hides
inside the nearest firewall.

Sultry Hooves

Murderous parrots eat souls
because of some old mummy's
full-flavoured horseplay.

Half-insane topers
bake a wine empire
in a wood oven.

Green Alexander stretches mud
grain by grain.

Mad Ephesians keep a watch.

A wholesome centaur ripens
an abstract word.

Horrible dark wings are found,
fit and unwearied.

Pictures of love gather
at the margin of work.

In a barrel
limbs swing
into a long Saturnian sleep.

Automatic Cabaret

Mannequins kiss robots
on starfish verandas,
royal supper boxes
jackknife in the aisle.

The cabaret lantern is lit,
the audition pit glistens,
slowly the spotlight comes
to a standstill.

The wind blows leaves
across the empty stage,
an absurd instinct
becomes a magic trick.

Greenroom gestures
rehearse the curtain call,
honkytonk atoms
shackle and whine,
a sculpted head
explodes in the lobby—
the price of world peace
has just gone up.

Route

Warred are we,
Between aqueducts we transport fire,
Between walls we design light.
We are attacked by something putrid,
Something bourgeois,
Something always wanting more.
Inert, we commission icons,
We assassinate at will;
Ever homeward bound,
Our writing is automatic.
Seven goats for the grey house ballet,
Eight horses for the deconstruction work,
A few pennies for burning our cars and shutting up—
There is a route
Out of here.

Chiang Mai

The fountains spread their wings,
a stopped clock strikes the hour.

Under a gateway the moat flashes,
old city anchors raise their glasses
like bridges to the moon.

The fountain spray forms
into something novel, it sails
past ancient walls, surfing waves
through weirs of tomorrow's pain.

Chiang Mai will win this battle and this war.
Nothing stale will be refreshed again.

IV.

Easy to Find

Found

One day it will be there, easy to find.

Don't expect any kind of fanfare.

There will be no firebird chorus
In silver-tint wind.

One day it appears, or you create it,
Or it creates you or itself
By appearing,
Or by being created by you.

Again: don't expect any kind of fanfare,
It will simply be there, easy to find.

In a Mountain Dream

In a mountain dream
I am by the blue mountain.
It is morning and I feel the cool mountain wind.
I seek the river, but I am lost.
A woman walks down from the mountain.
I greet her and ask her where the river is.
Instead of answering she tells me her name is Nadja.
I am named after the book, she says.
In the distance I see the blue mountain
because now I am with Nadja by the river,
walking in sunlight, listening to the buzz of insects.
The past remains up for grabs, she says,
including more than the light, the water, and the matter.
Speaking of water, she adds, have you had enough
of the river? Yes, I say, and I explain
my feelings about mountains.
I understand, she says. Then I am with her
by the blue mountain again.
Now I know where the river is,
now the breeze is warm and gentle.
Nadja is trying to catch a butterfly with a net.
And something else, she shouts, laughing:
There are accidental encounters
tramped all over the rules of the game.

Cairo Calling

A sparrow hawk steals
a dead ibis
from a kite's mouth.

An initiation text
acts as a talisman.
Magic words resound
in an inner world.
Exorcised spirits are kept at bay,
the bandaged life-force is healed.

Outside the city,
there is an obscure sign,
a fog that lights the way.

A Pharaoh's ghost castles
on the queen's side.

The Water Fire

for Nisthula Murphy

See the water fire,
Blue white yellow orange red,
It creates itself from nothing:
Alive it burn-flows and alive it flow-burns.

With wet dry wave-flames
And dry wet flame-waves
The water fire preserves itself:
It is a continuous affair.

The water fire is a part of time,
Part of desire passing through time
And of time passing through desire:
It is eternal.

The water fire quenches itself,
It is immune from any dearth of reality:
Creating, preserving, destroying,
Never and always at once.

Warm Abstraction

A bloodline reaches out for a frame
but the canvas boundary holds firm,
a dancer's hand grasps at nothing
and receives a small gypsy bird,
a word pushes back against reason
with a crystal bowl display,
a painting emits a yellow tone,
the sound is like a ballet.

A wood carving plays in the river sand
in flight from what has gone before,
a violin tells some half-truths
about a pigment's mad source,
an idea finds its opposite
in the silence of a whisper,
and warm abstraction supersedes,
with great finality, her cold sister.

Psilocybin

A silken clay courage casts a net
from the house of fear.

The guild stops to sigh
but the village does not waver.

From afar a voice is heard:
"Let all the humiliations
be desecrated."

Flea market élan
takes its chance:
dead secrets are saved
from a fever ravine.

In the mirror
an El Greco face is pulled—
it feels like Ecstatic Surrender.

Tinkling Wound

Late August. The cornfields are bruised by tar, the hayfields are glutted with green juice. The river's hips have become a thickened swamp, its spine a swan's throat. The hooded grain is inked, shielded from the sun. Pepper grass vents in the stinking mud. The bog burns inwards.

A knot of horns lie vivid in the shrunken byre. A cache of wet fruit glistens on top of a hoarded milk can. A fermented purse makes a sign of lust, the twisted tongue flesh perfected. The rat-grey victim smells and scratches a big red egg. His nails are slashed berries, his palms dark jam-pots. The ridge's hard chin is a forceps. Hope arrested, memory stained.

Raise the hands of heavy hunger, the wrists of round rain. Hang the sour shoulders, the rusted heels. The basalt fur on summer's sticky visor fills with opaque rot. The root beauty of a glossy oak can tan purple turf, a photograph of repose can cure a foetus's tinkling wound.

One Current of Rain

Meet the phantom avalanche,
the breathing convulsions.
Sense the make-believe little insects,
their furnaces on the pretend seashore.
Enjoy the clairvoyant signposts,
the scrubland imputations.
See how the journey inward misses nothing,
not even skinfuls of roses from afar.

Hear the wild form of monologue desire,
the loose form of mythological night,
it's all one current of rain, it's the light
behind the dark star, it's the shadow
behind the beatitude—
it's the lucid love you've been waiting for.

The Red Poppies Run to Us

By sunflowers near the periphery
dead prophets gather
to hear an older order speak.
They feel the past darken
beneath a thousand-yard stare.

By wildflowers near the hub
idle oracles convene
to see a new order fade.
There are blood spots on the grass,
lifebuoys on the green sea.

Slowly life is mistaken
for a tangent thrown away.
A symbolic fury rumbles,
the red poppies run to us,
reality thuds into being.

In a Recurring Dream

In a recurring dream
someone has been murdered.
I do not know who
but I know
I am the murderer.
It is an irreversible fact:
I did the deed.
I feel regret
but it is not clear if this is because
of the murder
or because
I am being hunted.
I am in a train compartment.
With me, a woman with straw-coloured hair.
Outside, a crimson horizon.
I know the woman is Nadja
and I know she knows
what is happening.
As the train speeds along,
Nadja hands me a picture of a painting.
It is *Centauro morente* by Giorgio de Chirico.
I tell her that I know the painting.
I see again the blue eyes
and the red wound
on the dying centaur's forehead.
I see the living centaur,
the one walking away,
his strong back and hind;

his determined air,
dark and nonchalant.
Unlike the rocky murder scene,
the sky is delicate,
yet this is an image
of a dead dream screaming
in the face of life.
I look up to say this
to Nadja
but she is no longer there.

Positive Outlook

The tropical haze, savage and tender,
records a nightmare.
The jungle's soft edge
reveals thoughts automatically.

As a fable turns a corner,
the equator closes its eye;
as a ritual reads a palm,
the forest defers.

The plantation's wild monotony
repeats its offer of eruption.
Retired subversive reason
hypnotizes its own groggy corpse.

The day's door is on offer,
an object finds a way.
The canopy exhales,
an anti-moment breaks through.

Heal

This ink runs its course,
As do wind and stone—
Mark the cave,
Scratch the wall.

Fight for your lifeline,
For your hopeful fear;
Fight for it, win it,
Be with it, run with it.

This energy finds light,
As do sound and space—
Paint the violet sky,
Draw the silent island.

Breach the surface,
The template of harmony;
Heal your heart,
Wake your sleeping dream.

Notes

The title, "Mouth of Shadows", comes from Victor Hugo's poem, "Ce que dit la bouche d'ombre" ["What the Mouth of Shadows Says"], first published in Hugo's collection, *Les Contemplations* (Michel Lévy et Pagnerre, 1856). For Hugo and for early twentieth-century French surrealists including André Breton, Philippe Soupault, and Louis Aragon, the expression referred to the unconscious.

The idea of "identity confiscation" in the poem "Mouth of Shadows" is from Habib Tengour's manifesto, "Le surréalisme maghrébin" ["Maghrebi Surrealism"], first published in 1981 in the magazine, *Peuples Méditerranéens*.

"Hidden Bow" is a cut-up of the English translation, by Stephen Kessler and Lewis Hyde, of "El silencio" ["Silence"] by Vicente Aleixandre. The poem is from Aleixandre's collection, *Pasión de la tierra* [*The Earth's Passion*] (Fábula, 1935). The translation used here is from *A Longing for the Light: Selected Poems of Vicente Aleixandre* (Copper Canyon Press, 1979), edited by Lewis Hyde.

"Backing Vocal" includes lyrics from the 1965 single, "King of the Road", written and performed by Roger Miller and released on the Smash label.

"Injured Beach Star" is a cut-up of the English versions of three poems by André Breton: the translations of "Personnage blessé" ["Injured Person"] and "Femmes sur la plage" ["Women on the Beach"] by Jean-Pierre Cauvin, and the translation of "L'Etoile matinale" ["Morning Star"] by Mary Ann Caws. All three are from

Breton's collection of prose poems, *Constellations* (Pierre Matisse Gallery, 1959). The translations used here are from *Poems of André Breton: A Bilingual Anthology* (Black Widow Press, 2006), translated and edited by Jean-Pierre Cauvin and Mary Ann Caws.

"The Great Ships" is a cut-up of the English translations, by Lewis Hyde, of "Mi voz" ["My Voice"] and "Siempre" ["The Usual"] by Vicente Aleixandre. The poems are from Aleixandre's collection, *Espados como labios* [*Swords Like Lips*] (Espasa Calpe, 1932). The translations used here are from *A Longing for the Light: Selected Poems of Vicente Aleixandre* (Copper Canyon Press, 1979), edited by Lewis Hyde.

The epigraph to "Minotaur in Green" is from Joyce Mansour's poem, "Pandémonium", in her collection of the same name (La Nueva Foglio, 1976). The English version given here is from Katharine Conley's translation of the poem in the journal, *Dada/Surrealism*, No. 19 (2013).

"Bound Composition" is a response to an exercise suggested in the chapter, "Stray Thoughts on Roethke and Teaching", in Richard Hugo's book, *The Triggering Town* (WW Norton & Company, 1979).

"Painted Canvases" is modelled after Noelle Kocot's poem, "Tongues", in *Humanity* (SurVision Books, 2018).

"Apple Graves" is a cut-up of the English translation, by Greg Simon and Steven F. White, of "Pasaje de la multitude que orina (Nocturno de Battery Place)" ["Landscape of a Pissing Multitude (Battery Place Nocturne)"] by Federico García Lorca. The poem is from Lorca's posthumous collection, *Poeta en Nueva York* [*Poet in New York*] (Editorial Séneca, 1940). The translation used here is from Christopher Maurer's bilingual edition published by Farrar Straus Giroux in 1988.

"Barricades of Pain" is a cut-up of two poems by Oscar Wilde: "Sonnet to Liberty" and "Sonnet Written in Holy Week at Genoa". Both are included in Wilde's collection, *Poems* (David Bogue, 1881).

"Sultry Hooves" is a cut-up of "On a Picture of a Black Centaur by Edmund Dulac" by William Butler Yeats. The poem is from Yeats's collection, *The Tower*, first published in 1928 by Macmillan & Co.

"In a Mountain Dream" is modelled after the dream poems in Richard Hugo's collection, *31 Letters and 13 Dreams* (WW Norton & Company, 1977).

"Tinkling Wound" is a cut-up of two poems by Seamus Heaney: "Blackberry-Picking", from *Death of a Naturalist* (Faber and Faber, 1966), and "The Grauballe Man", from *North* (Faber and Faber, 1975).

Selected Poetry Titles Published by SurVision Books

Seeds of Gravity: An Anthology of Contemporary Surrealist Poetry from Ireland
Edited by Anatoly Kudryavitsky
ISBN 978-1-912963-18-8

Invasion: An Anthology of Ukrainian Poetry about the War
Edited by Tony Kitt
ISBN 978-1-912963-32-4

Noelle Kocot. *Humanity*
(New Poetics: USA)
ISBN 978-1-9995903-0-7

Marc Vincenz. *Einstein Fledermaus*
(New Poetics: USA)
ISBN 978-1-912963-20-1

Helen Ivory. *Maps of the Abandoned City*
(New Poetics: England)
ISBN 978-1-912963-04-1

Tony Kitt. *The Magic Phlute*
(New Poetics: Ireland)
ISBN 978-1-912963-08-9

Tim Murphy. *The Cacti Do Not Move*
(New Poetics: Ireland)
ISBN 978-1-912963-07-2

John W. Sexton. *Inverted Night*
(New Poetics: Ireland)
ISBN 978-1-912963-05-8

Aoife Mannix. *Alice under the Knife*
  (Winner of James Tate Poetry Prize 2020)
  ISBN 978-1-912963-26-3

Tony Bailie. *Mountain Under Heaven*
  (Winner of James Tate Poetry Prize 2019)
  ISBN 978-1-912963-09-6

Michelle Moloney King. *Another Word for Mother*
  (New Poetics: Ireland)
  ISBN 978-1-912963-31-7

Matthew Geden. *Fruit*
  (New Poetics: Ireland)
  ISBN 978-1-912963-16-4

Afric McGlinchey. *Invisible Insane*
  (New Poetics: Ireland)
  ISBN 978-1-9995903-3-8

Charles Borkhuis. *Spontaneous Combustion*
  (Winner of James Tate Poetry Prize 2021)
  ISBN 978-1-912963-30-0

Ciaran O'Driscoll. *Angel Hour*
  ISBN 978-1-912963-27-0

George Kalamaras. *That Moment of Wept*
  ISBN 978-1-9995903-7-6

George Kalamaras. *Through the Silk-Heavy Rains*
  ISBN 978-1-912963-28-7

Order our books from http://survisionmagazine.com/bookshop.htm